SCRAPPY & HAPPY QUILTS

LIMITED PALETTE, TONS OF FUN!

KATE HENDERSON

Martingale®
Create with Confidence

Scrappy & Happy Quilts: Limited Palette, Tons of Fun!
© 2018 by Kate Henderson

Martingale®
19021 120th Ave. NE, Ste. 102
Bothell, WA 98011-9511 USA
ShopMartingale.com

Printed in China
23 22 21 20 19 18   8 7 6 5 4 3 2 1

**Library of Congress Cataloging-in-Publication Data
is available upon request.**

ISBN: 978-1-60468-862-7

MISSION STATEMENT

We empower makers who use fabric and yarn
to make life more enjoyable.

CREDITS

PUBLISHER AND
CHIEF VISIONARY OFFICER
Jennifer Erbe Keltner

CONTENT DIRECTOR
Karen Costello Soltys

DESIGN MANAGER
Adrienne Smitke

MANAGING EDITOR
Tina Cook

PRODUCTION MANAGER
Regina Girard

ACQUISITIONS EDITOR
Karen M. Burns

PHOTOGRAPHER
Brent Kane

TECHNICAL EDITOR
Nancy Mahoney

ILLUSTRATOR
Lisa Lauch

COPY EDITOR
Durby Peterson

SPECIAL THANKS
*Thanks to Sara and Thomas Kappler of Kirkland, Washington,
for allowing us to photograph this book in their home.*

DEDICATION

*To my parents, Christina and Keith, who have always
supported and encouraged me in everything I've wanted to do.*

CONTENTS

INTRODUCTION

Without a doubt, color is my favorite part of quilting. Actually, color is my favorite part of everything. My house and wardrobe look like a rainbow exploded; the only things that are plain in my house are the walls, and that's so I can cover them in quilts and paintings. So it was quite odd when I found myself being drawn to vintage blue-and-white and red-and-white quilts. I couldn't get them out of my mind, so I tried making a few blocks. As hard as I tried to stick to just two solid colors, the designs needed additional prints or a bit of a different color. The results are the 13 quilts in this book. Most are scrappy, some use combinations of solids and prints, and a couple use just a few fabrics, but even with a limited color palette, all of them are full of color.

The first half of the book features quilts with just two colors, and the second half has quilts that are three colors. Of course you can choose your favorite color and get sewing, but don't forget to experiment with colors you don't normally use, and also combine the unexpected to make each quilt your own.

HAPPY QUILTING!

FABRICS & COLOR SCHEMES

One of the best parts of quiltmaking is choosing the fabric. I love to spend an hour or two playing around with fabric, making piles of different color and print combinations. I'm no expert on color, but I know what I like and I'm not afraid to experiment with different combinations. In this section, you'll find some of my ways of choosing quilt fabrics, but ultimately it's up to you. If you like the fabrics and colors you've chosen, then they're perfect!

BACKGROUND FABRICS

The background fabric you choose can dramatically change the look of your quilt. Solids, especially white or cream, are always a go-to option for me. I use a lot of bright colors, and a white background makes them pop. A really dark gray or navy can do the same thing.

If you want something a little different for your background, low-volume fabrics are a good option. Low-volume fabrics read as light fabrics but at the same time have a secondary pattern or design. A low-volume fabric could be white, cream, or pale gray.

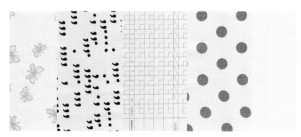

From a distance, low-volume fabrics often read as solid, but up close they're more interesting than a solid.

SOLID FABRICS

The majority of my stash is made up of prints, but my collection of solids is increasing. Most manufacturers have a range of solids that coordinate with their prints, and solids come in every color you could wish for.

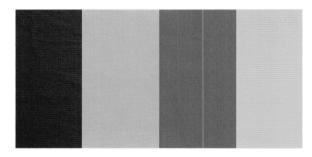

Solids mix perfectly with prints in a scrappy quilt, and they can also work as the main feature in a quilt.

COLOR SCHEMES

Color schemes are logical combinations of colors on a color wheel. A color wheel is a helpful tool for determining color combinations that will work well together. A basic color scheme uses two colors that look appealing when paired.

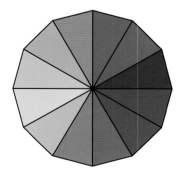

Monotone

For a monotone color scheme, choose one color you like and add different shades and tints of that color. Add solids and prints that are darker and lighter. Then add brighter and more muted fabrics. The prints can be composed of many colors; they just need to read as your chosen color from a distance.

If choosing colors and playing with different combinations fills you with dread, start by focusing on a monotone color scheme.

Analogous

Analogous colors are next to each other on the color wheel. For an analogous color scheme, first select fabrics of a single color. Then add two more colors, the ones that—on the color wheel—lie on either side of the first.

Because the colors blend together, quilts with analogous color schemes have a calming effect.

Complementary

Complementary colors are opposite each other on the color wheel—for example, red and green, purple and yellow, or blue and orange. They are happy and bright combinations that will cheer you up even in the depths of winter. I'm a big fan of lots of color, so I love these combinations. But if you find them a bit jarring, consider a pastel version, such as a pairing of pale pinks and greens. Or use one color as the main color and add small amounts of its complementary color, as I did in Between the Lines on page 61. The main color of that quilt is orange, and I included pops of blue to add interest.

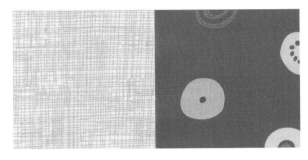

Choosing mint rather than a vibrant green calms down this complementary pairing.

Blue and Gray

My go-to colors are blue and gray, like the dove and navy solids shown below. I find that they work with every other color.

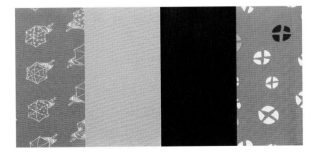

If there's a color you want to use but you can't decide what color to include with it, try a blue or a gray.

PINK DAISY

Daisies have always been my favorite flowers, and their cheery look inspired this design. I made a big square quilt, but if you use 2½" squares instead of 4" squares as I did, you'll have a baby or wall quilt.

MATERIALS

Yardage is based on 42"-wide fabric.

3 yards *total* of assorted pink prints for squares and binding

2½ yards of white solid for background

4¼ yards of fabric for backing

75" × 75" square of batting

CUTTING

Label the pieces as indicated in parentheses.

From the pink prints, cut a *total* of:

19 strips, 4" × 42"; crosscut into 168 squares, 4" × 4"

2½"-wide strips in various lengths to total 290" when joined end to end

From the white solid, cut:

20 strips, 4" × 42"; crosscut into:

    4 rectangles, 4" × 18" (A)

    12 rectangles, 4" × 14½" (B)

    4 rectangles, 4" × 11" (C)

    42 rectangles, 4" × 7½" (D)

    29 squares, 4" × 4" (E)

ASSEMBLING THE QUILT TOP

Press all seam allowances as indicated by the arrows.

1 For rows 1–9, lay out pink squares, white rectangles, and white squares as shown below. Sew the pieces together into rows. Make two of each row. The rows should measure 4" × 67".

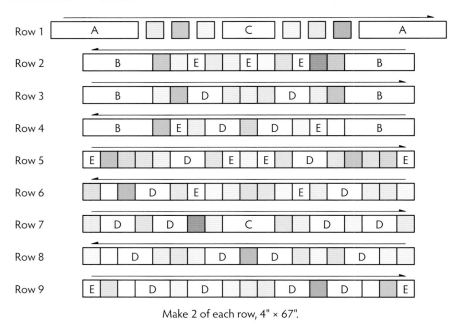

Make 2 of each row, 4" × 67".

2 For row 10, join two white D rectangles, three white squares, and 12 pink squares to make a 4" × 67" row.

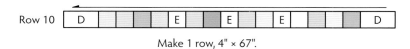

Make 1 row, 4" × 67".

USING A DESIGN WALL

I find it useful to lay out the pieces on a design wall when making a quilt like this one. Being able to stand back and assess how the fabrics are arranged helps me avoid any fabric-placement errors.

3 Lay out rows 1–10 as shown in the quilt assembly diagram below. Join the rows to complete the quilt top, which should measure 67" square.

4 Stitch around the perimeter of the quilt top, ⅛" from the outer edges, to lock the seams in place.

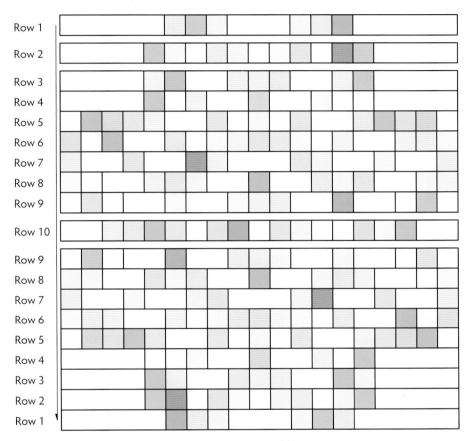

Quilt assembly

FINISHING THE QUILT

For help with the following finishing steps, go to ShopMartingale.com/HowtoQuilt for free, illustrated instructions.

1 Layer the quilt top, batting, and backing; baste the layers together. Hand or machine quilt. I free-motion quilted loops and flowers across the quilt.

2 Join the pink 2½"-wide strips to make a strip at least 290" long. Use the pieced strip to bind the edges of the quilt. Add a label if desired.

HAPPY STARS

FINISHED QUILT: 68" × 68" | FINISHED BLOCK: 13½" × 13½"

*I can't help but smile when I sew with yellow. It is the happiest
of colors. Can't decide between using solids or prints? Use both!*

MATERIALS

*Yardage is based on 42"-wide fabric. Fat quarters are
18" × 21". To learn how I allocated the various yellow
prints and solids, see "Fabric Selection" on page 14.*

10 fat quarters of assorted yellow prints for blocks
⅝ yard *each* of 3 yellow solids for blocks
¾ yard *each* of 2 yellow solids for blocks
1¼ yards of white solid for blocks
⅝ yard of yellow solid for binding
4¼ yards of fabric for backing
76" × 76" square of batting

CUTTING

From *each* of 5 yellow prints, cut:
1 strip, 5½" × 21"; crosscut into 2 squares,
    5½" × 5½" (10 total)
1 strip, 5" × 21"; crosscut into 4 squares, 5" × 5"
    (20 total)

From *each* of the 5 remaining yellow prints, cut:
2 strips, 5" × 21"; crosscut into:
    2 rectangles, 5" × 14" (10 total)
    2 squares, 5" × 5" (10 total)
1 strip, 2½" × 21"; crosscut into:
    2 squares, 2½" × 2½" (10 total)
    4 squares, 2" × 2" (20 total)

From *each* of the 3 yellow solids, cut:
1 strip, 5½" × 42"; crosscut into 4 squares,
    5½" × 5½" (12 total)
2 strips, 5" × 42"; crosscut into:
    2 rectangles, 5" × 14" (6 total)
    10 squares, 5" × 5" (30 total)
1 strip, 2½" × 42"; crosscut into:
    2 squares, 2½" × 2½" (6 total)
    4 squares, 2" × 2" (12 total)

From *each* of the 2 yellow solids, cut:
1 strip, 5½" × 42"; crosscut into 2 squares,
    5½" × 5½" (4 total)
3 strips, 5" × 42"; crosscut into:
    4 rectangles, 5" × 14" (8 total)
    8 squares, 5" × 5" (16 total)
1 strip, 2½" × 42"; crosscut into:
    4 squares, 2½" × 2½" (8 total)
    8 squares, 2" × 2" (16 total)

From the white solid, cut:
4 strips, 5½" × 42"; crosscut into 26 squares,
    5½" × 5½"
2 strips, 5" × 42"; crosscut into 13 squares, 5" × 5"
2 strips, 2½" × 42"; crosscut into 24 squares,
    2½" × 2½"
1 strip, 2" × 42"; crosscut into 12 squares, 2" × 2"

From the yellow solid for binding, cut:
8 strips, 2½" × 42"

FABRIC SELECTION

You'll have three different groups of yellow fabric for your blocks, and here's how they're allocated. Out of ten yellow fat quarters, five are for Large Star blocks and the other five are for Small Star blocks. The group of three yellow solids are for six Large Star and three Small Star blocks. The remaining two yellow solids are for two Large Star and four Small Star blocks, for a total of 13 Large and 12 Small Star blocks.

MAKING THE LARGE STAR BLOCKS

For each block, choose two 5½" squares and four 5" squares, all from one yellow fabric, plus two white 5½" squares and one white 5" square. Instructions are for making one block. Repeat the steps to make a total of 13 blocks. Press all seam allowances as indicated by the arrows.

1 Referring to "Half-Square-Triangle Units" on page 78, pair a white 5½" square with a yellow 5½" square to make two half-square-triangle units. Trim the units to measure 5" square. Make four matching units.

Make 4 units.

2 Join two yellow 5" squares and one half-square-triangle unit, making sure to orient the unit as shown. Make two matching units measuring 5" × 14", including the seam allowances.

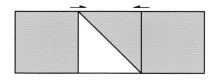

Make 2 units, 5" × 14".

3 Join two half-square-triangle units from step 1 and one white 5" square, making sure to orient the units as shown. Make one unit measuring 5" × 14", including the seam allowances.

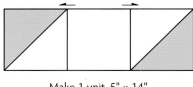

Make 1 unit, 5" × 14".

4 Join the units from steps 2 and 3 together as shown to complete one block. Make a total of 13 blocks measuring 14" square, including the seam allowances.

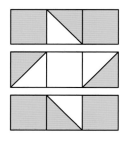 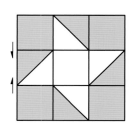

Make 13 blocks,
14" × 14".

MAKING THE SMALL STAR BLOCKS

For each block, choose two 5" × 14" rectangles, two 5" squares, two 2½" squares, and four 2" squares, all from one yellow fabric, plus two white 2½" squares and one white 2" square. Instructions are for making one block. Repeat the steps to make a total of 12 blocks. Press all seam allowances as indicated by the arrows.

1 Referring to "Half-Square-Triangle Units," pair a white 2½" square with a yellow 2½" square to make two half-square-triangle units. Trim the units to measure 2" square. Make four matching units.

2 Repeat steps 2–4 of "Making the Large Star Blocks" on page 14 to make one small star unit measuring 5" square, including the seam allowances.

3 Sew yellow 5" squares to opposite sides of the star unit to make the center row. The row should measure 5" × 14", including the seam allowances.

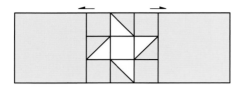

4 Sew yellow 5" × 14" rectangles to the top and bottom of the center row to complete one Small Star block. Make a total of 12 blocks measuring 14" square, including the seam allowances.

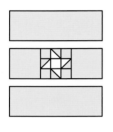 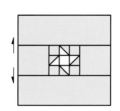

Make 12 blocks,
14" × 14".

ASSEMBLING THE QUILT TOP

1 Arrange the blocks in five rows of five blocks each, alternating the Large and Small Star blocks as shown in the quilt assembly diagram below. Sew the blocks together into rows. Join the rows to complete the quilt top. The quilt top should measure 68" square.

2 Stitch around the perimeter of the quilt top, ⅛" from the outer edges, to lock the seams in place.

FINISHING THE QUILT

For help with the following finishing steps, go to ShopMartingale.com/HowtoQuilt for free, illustrated instructions.

1 Layer the quilt top, batting, and backing; baste the layers together. Hand or machine quilt. I free-motion quilted swirly lines with stars across the quilt.

2 Using the yellow 2½"-wide strips, bind the edges of the quilt. Add a label if desired.

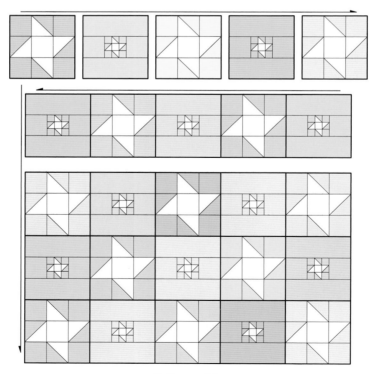

Quilt assembly

DAY AT THE BEACH

A quilt of calming pale blue and aqua reminds me of my favorite summer days spent building sand castles and jumping through waves in the beautiful Indian Ocean.

MATERIALS

Yardage is based on 42"-wide fabric.

3½ yards of white solid for background

1¾ yards *total* of assorted aqua and blue prints for units and binding (referred to collectively as "aqua")

4 yards of fabric for backing

69" × 69" square of batting

CUTTING

From the white solid, cut:

9 strips, 4" × 42"; crosscut into 80 squares, 4" × 4"

19 strips, 3½" × 42"; crosscut 8 *of the strips* into:
    2 strips, 3½" × 36½"
    2 strips, 3½" × 30½"
    2 strips, 3½" × 24½"
    2 strips, 3½" × 18½"
    8 squares, 3½" × 3½"

1 square, 12½" × 12½"

From the aqua prints, cut a *total* of:

80 squares, 4" × 4"

8 squares, 3½" × 3½"

2½"-wide strips in various lengths to total 255" when joined end to end

MAKING THE CENTER UNIT

Press all seam allowances as indicated by the arrows.

1 Referring to "Half-Square-Triangle Units" on page 78, pair a white 4" square with an aqua 4" square to make two half-square-triangle units. Trim the units to measure 3½" square. Make a total of 160 units.

Make 160 units.

2 Join four half-square-triangle units, making sure to orient them as shown. Make two units measuring 3½" × 12½", including the seam allowances.

Make 2 units,
3½" × 12½".

3 Join four half-square-triangle units, one aqua 3½" square, and one white 3½" square as shown. Make two strips measuring 3½" × 18½", including the seam allowances.

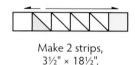

Make 2 strips,
3½" × 18½".

4 Sew the strips from step 2 to opposite sides of the white 12½" square. Sew the strips from step 3 to the top and bottom of the square. The unit should measure 18½" square, including the seam allowances.

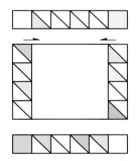 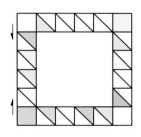

5 Sew white 3½" × 18½" strips to opposite sides of the unit from step 4. Sew white 3½" × 24½" strips to the top and bottom of the unit. Press the seam allowances toward the white strips. The unit should measure 24½" square, including the seam allowances.

6 Join eight half-square-triangle units, making sure to orient them as shown. Make two strips measuring 3½" × 24½", including the seam allowances.

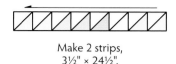

Make 2 strips,
3½" × 24½".

7 Join eight half-square-triangle units, one aqua 3½" square, and one white 3½" square as shown. Make two strips measuring 3½" × 30½", including the seam allowances.

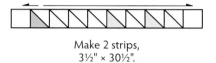

Make 2 strips,
3½" × 30½".

8 Sew the strips from step 6 to opposite sides of the unit from step 5. Sew the strips from step 7 to the top and bottom of the unit from step 5. The unit should measure 30½" square, including the seam allowances.

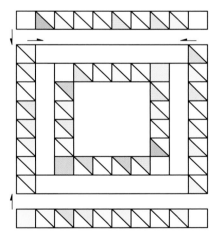

9 Sew white 3½" × 30½" strips to opposite sides of the unit from step 8. Sew white 3½" × 36½" strips to the top and bottom of the unit. Press the seam allowances toward the white strips. The quilt-top center should measure 36½" square, including the seam allowances.

COMPLETING THE QUILT TOP

Refer to the quilt assembly diagram on page 21 for placement guidance throughout.

1 Join 12 half-square-triangle units, making sure to orient them as shown. Make two strips measuring 3½" × 36½", including the seam allowances.

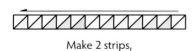

Make 2 strips,
3½" × 36½".

2 Join 12 half-square-triangle units, one aqua 3½" square, and one white 3½" square as shown. Make two strips measuring 3½" × 42½", including the seam allowances.

Make 2 strips,
3½" × 42½".

3 Sew the strips from step 1 to opposite sides of the quilt top. Sew the strips from step 2 to the top and bottom of the quilt top. The quilt top should measure 42½" square, including the seam allowances.

4 Join five white 3½" × 42" strips end to end. From the pieced strip, cut two 48½"-long strips and two 42½"-long strips. Sew the 42½"-long strips to opposite sides of the quilt top. Sew the 48½"-long strips to the top and bottom of the quilt top. The quilt top should measure 48½" square, including the seam allowances.

5 Join 16 half-square-triangle units, making sure to orient them as shown. Make two strips measuring 3½" × 48½", including the seam allowances.

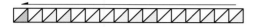

Make 2 strips,
3½" × 48½".

6 Join 16 half-square-triangle units, one aqua 3½" square, and one white 3½" square as shown. Make two strips measuring 3½" × 54½", including the seam allowances.

Make 2 strips,
3½" × 54½".

7 Sew the strips from step 5 to opposite sides of the quilt top. Sew the strips from step 6 to the top and bottom. The quilt top should measure 54½" square, including the seam allowances.

8 Join the remaining six white 3½" × 42" strips end to end. From the pieced strip, cut two 54½"-long strips and two 60½"-long strips. Sew the 54½"-long strips to opposite sides of the quilt top. Sew the 60½"-long strips to the top and bottom of the quilt top. The quilt top should measure 60½" square.

FINISHING THE QUILT

For help with the following finishing steps, go to ShopMartingale.com/HowtoQuilt for free, illustrated instructions.

1 Layer the quilt top, batting, and backing; baste the layers together. Hand or machine quilt. I free-motion quilted an allover echoing spiky pattern across the quilt.

2 Join the aqua 2½"-wide strips to make a strip at least 255" long. Use the pieced strip to bind the edges of the quilt. Add a label if desired.

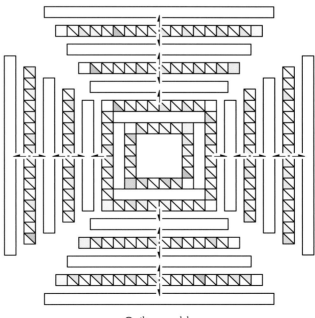

Quilt assembly

POPPIES

With bright red fabrics and a clever arrangement, the simple Drunkard's Path block is transformed into a wonderful spring garden.

MATERIALS

Yardage is based on 42"-wide fabric. Fat quarters are 18" × 21".

4⅞ yards of white print for background

¾ yard *each* of 3 assorted red prints for blocks and binding

1 fat quarter *each* of 6 assorted red prints for blocks and binding

4¾ yards of fabric for backing

81" × 81" square of batting

Template plastic

CUTTING

Referring to "Templates" on page 76, trace patterns A–D on pages 26 and 27 onto template plastic, cut them out, and use them to cut the pieces listed below.

From the white print, cut:

6 strips, 12½" × 42"; crosscut into 18 squares, 12½" × 12½"

36 of template A

12 of template B

72 of template C

24 of template D

From *each* of the 3 red prints, cut:

4 of template A (12 total)

12 of template B (36 total)

2 strips, 2½" × 42"; cut in half to yield 12 strips, 2½" × 21" (2 will be extra)

From *each* of the 6 red print fat quarters, cut:

4 of template C (24 total)

12 of template D (72 total)

1 strip, 2½" × 21" (6 total)

MAKING THE BLOCKS

Press all seam allowances as indicated by the arrows.

1   Fold a white A piece and a red B piece in half and finger-press to mark the center of each piece. Pin piece A on top of piece B, right sides together, matching the center creases and easing the fabrics to fit. Sew the pieces together. Make three sets of 12 matching units (36 total) measuring 6½" square, including the seam allowances.

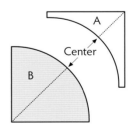

Make 36 units,
6½" × 6½".

2 Repeat step 1 using a red A piece and a white B piece. Make three sets of four matching units (12 total).

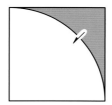

Make 12 units,
6½" × 6½".

3 Arrange three units from step 1 and one unit from step 2, all from the same print, in two rows. Sew the units together into rows. Join the rows to make a quadrant. Make three sets of four matching quadrants (12 total) measuring 12½" square, including the seam allowances.

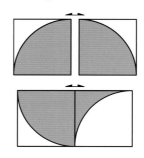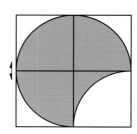

Make 12 units,
12½" × 12½".

4 Arrange four matching quadrants from step 3 in two rows. Sew the quadrants together into rows. Join the rows to complete one large Poppy block. Make three blocks measuring 24½" square, including the seam allowances.

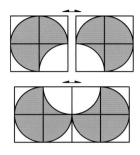 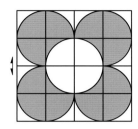

Make 3 blocks,
24½" × 24½".

5 Repeat steps 1–4 using red and white C and D pieces to make six small Poppy blocks measuring 12½" square, including the seam allowances.

Make 6 blocks,
12½" × 12½".

SCRAPPY BINDING

I love to use scraps left over from piecing my blocks for binding. I cut the scraps into 2½"-wide strips and then sew them together end to end to minimize waste (I prefer the look of straight seams, as opposed to diagonal seams, when using scraps for binding). To learn about a different kind of scrappy binding, see "Binding with a Contrast Strip" on page 62.

ASSEMBLING THE QUILT TOP

1 Arrange one large Poppy block, one small Poppy block, and four white 12½" squares as shown. Sew two white squares and the small Poppy block together to make the bottom row. Sew two white squares together; then add the large Poppy block to make the top row. Sew the rows together to make a section. Make three sections measuring 36½" square, including the seam allowances.

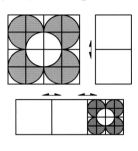 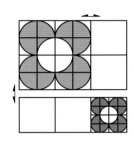

Make 3 sections,
36½" × 36½".

2 Arrange three small Poppy blocks and six white 12½" squares in three rows as shown. Sew the blocks and squares together into rows. Join the rows to make a section measuring 36½" square, including the seam allowances.

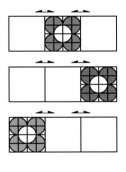 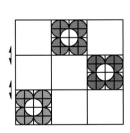

Make 1 section,
36½" × 36½".

3 Arrange the sections from steps 1 and 2 in two rows of two sections each as shown in the quilt assembly diagram on page 26. Sew the sections together into rows. Join the rows to complete the quilt top. The quilt top should measure 72½" square.

4 Stitch around the perimeter of the quilt top, ⅛" from the outer edges, to lock the seams in place.

FINISHING THE QUILT

For help with the following finishing steps, go to ShopMartingale.com/HowtoQuilt for free, illustrated instructions.

1 Layer the quilt top, batting, and backing; baste the layers together. Hand or machine quilt. I free-motion quilted whirly flowers across the quilt.

2 Join the red 2½"-wide strips to make a strip at least 305" long. Use the pieced strip to bind the edges of the quilt. Add a label if desired.

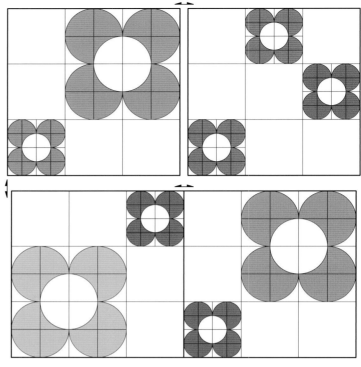

Quilt assembly

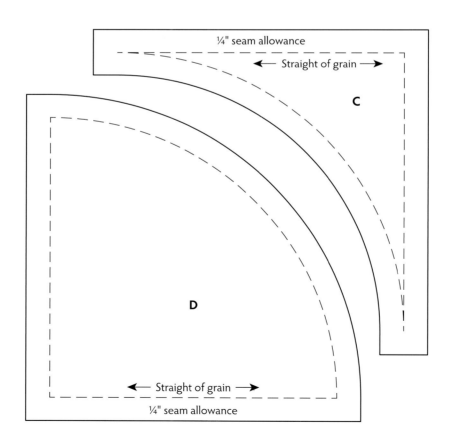

¼" seam allowance

← Straight of grain →

C

D

← Straight of grain →

¼" seam allowance

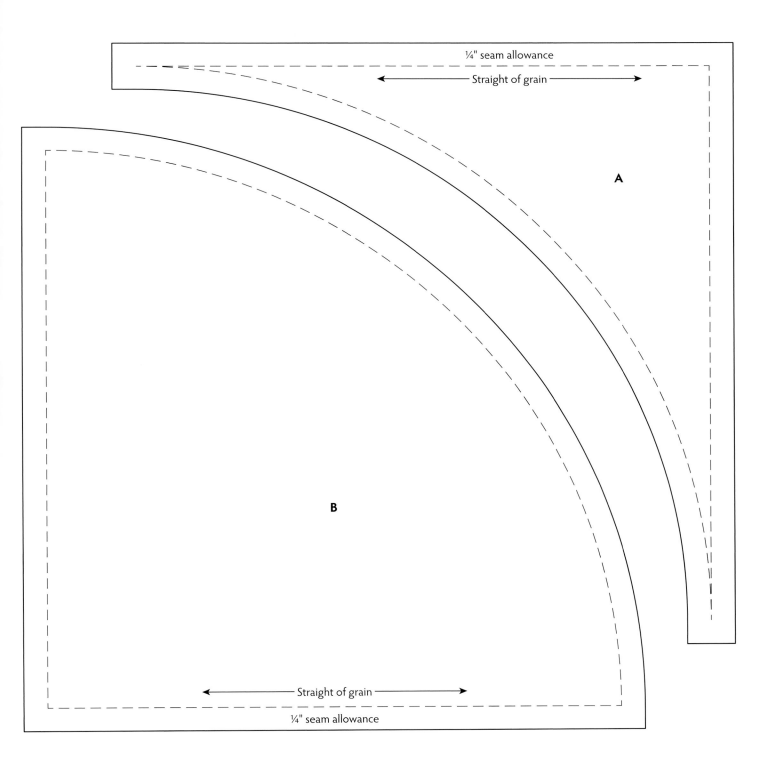

¼" seam allowance

Straight of grain

A

B

Straight of grain

¼" seam allowance

FIELDS OF GREEN

FINISHED QUILT: 60½" × 69½"

I love improvisational quilting, but it doesn't come naturally for me. I designed this quilt to have a scrappy improvisational look, although it's pieced in a structured way.

MATERIALS

Yardage is based on 42"-wide fabric.

4½ yards *total* of assorted green prints and solids for half-square-triangle units and background
⅝ yard of white solid for half-square-triangle units
⅝ yard of green print for binding
4⅛ yards of fabric for backing
69" × 78" piece of batting

CUTTING

Label the pieces as indicated in parentheses.

From the green prints and solids, cut a *total* of:
2 rectangles, 15½" × 18½" (L)
2 rectangles, 3½" × 18½" (I)
1 rectangle, 12½" × 15½" (M)
2 rectangles, 9½" × 15½" (N)
3 rectangles, 6½" × 15½" (F)
3 rectangles, 3½" × 15½" (D)
2 squares, 12½" × 12½" (A)
2 rectangles, 9½" × 12½" (E)
6 rectangles, 3½" × 12½" (B)
3 squares, 9½" × 9½" (H)
7 rectangles, 6½" × 9½" (G)
6 rectangles, 3½" × 9½" (J)
9 squares, 6½" × 6½" (C)
3 rectangles, 3½" × 6½" (K)
42 squares, 4" × 4"

From the white solid, cut:
5 strips, 4" × 42"; crosscut into 42 squares, 4" × 4"

From the green print for binding, cut:
7 strips, 2½" × 42"

MAKING THE FLYING GEESE

Press all seam allowances as indicated by the arrows.

1 Referring to "Half-Square-Triangle Units" on page 78, pair a green 4" square with a white square to make two half-square-triangle units. On one unit press the seam allowances toward the green triangle. On the other unit press the seam allowances toward the white triangle. Trim both units to measure 3½" square. Make 42 sets of two matching units.

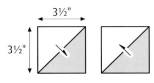

Make 42 of each unit.

2 Sew two matching units from step 1 together to make a flying-geese unit. Make 42 units measuring 3½" × 6½", including the seam allowances.

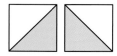
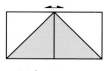

Make 42 units,
3½" × 6½".

3 Sew 14 units from step 2 together to make a strip. Make three strips measuring 6½" × 42½", including the seam allowances.

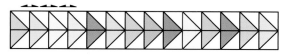

Make 3 strips,
6½" × 42½".

MAKING THE SECTIONS

Use the green rectangles and squares to make each section.

1 For section 1, lay out one A and three C squares and one each of B, D, E, F, G, and N rectangles. Join the squares and rectangles as shown to make a section measuring 12½" × 60½", including the seam allowances.

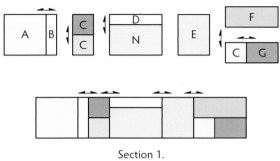

Section 1.
Make 1 section , 12½" × 60½".

2 For section 2, lay out one H square and three G, two B, and one each of I and J rectangles. Join the square, rectangles, and two flying-geese strips as shown to make a section measuring 15½" × 60½", including the seam allowances.

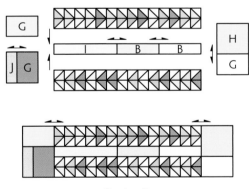

Section 2.
Make 1 section , 15½" × 60½".

3 For section 3, lay out one C square and one G, two each of J and K, and three B rectangles. Join the square, rectangles, and one flying-geese strip as shown to make a section measuring 9½" × 60½", including the seam allowances.

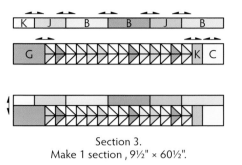

Section 3.
Make 1 section , 9½" × 60½".

4 For section 4, lay out one C square and two J and one each of F, G, and K rectangles. Join the square and rectangles as shown to make a section measuring 12½" × 21½", including the seam allowances.

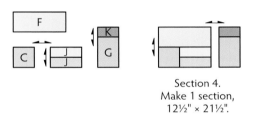

Section 4.
Make 1 section,
12½" × 21½".

5 For section 5, lay out two C squares and one each of D, G, and L rectangles. Join the squares and rectangles as shown to make a section measuring 21½" square, including the seam allowances.

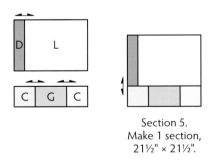

Section 5.
Make 1 section,
21½" × 21½".

6 For section 6, lay out one A square, two C squares, and one each of D, F, I, and M rectangles. Join the square and rectangles as shown to make a section measuring 15½" × 39½", including the seam allowances.

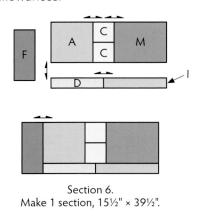

Section 6.
Make 1 section, 15½" × 39½".

7 For section 7, lay out two H squares and one each of E, J, L, and N rectangles. Join the squares and rectangles as shown to make a section measuring 18½" × 39½", including the seam allowances.

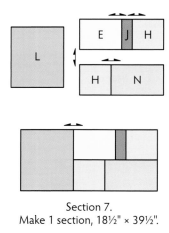

Section 7.
Make 1 section, 18½" × 39½".

ASSEMBLING THE QUILT TOP

1 Arrange the seven sections as shown in the quilt assembly diagram at right. Sew sections 1, 2, and 3 together along their long edges to make the top part of the quilt.

2 Join sections 4 and 5 to make the bottom-left section. Join sections 6 and 7 to make the bottom-right section. Join the left and right sections to make the bottom part of the quilt.

3 Join the top and bottom parts to complete the quilt top. The quilt top should measure 60½" × 69½".

4 Stitch around the perimeter of the quilt top, ⅛" from the outer edges, to lock the seams in place.

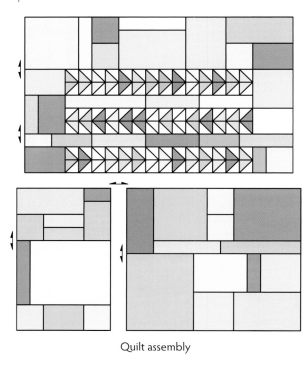

Quilt assembly

FINISHING THE QUILT

For help with the following finishing steps, go to ShopMartingale.com/HowtoQuilt for free, illustrated instructions.

1 Layer the quilt top, batting, and backing; baste the layers together. Hand or machine quilt. I free-motion quilted an allover motif of branches with leaves across the quilt.

2 Using the green 2½"-wide strips, bind the edges of the quilt. Add a label if desired.

SUNRISE

Sunrise is the perfect size for a wall hanging. With paper-foundation piecing you'll be able to stitch perfect points on the suns.

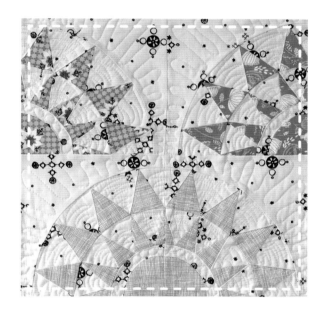

MATERIALS

Yardage is based on 42"-wide fabric. Fat quarters are 18"×21". Fat eighths are 9"×21".

2¾ yards of white print for background

8 fat quarters of assorted orange prints for blocks

4 fat eighths of assorted orange prints for blocks

⅜ yard of orange print for binding

1⅜ yards of fabric for backing

35" × 42" piece of batting

Template plastic

CUTTING

Referring to "Templates" on page 76, trace patterns A, B, and E on page 38 onto template plastic and cut them out. Use the templates to cut the pieces from the fabrics indicated below.

From the white print, cut:

10 strips, 3¼" × 42"; crosscut into 100 rectangles, 3¼" × 3¾"

7 strips, 2¾" × 42"; crosscut into 80 rectangles, 2¾" × 3¼"

20 of template B

20 of template E

From *each* orange print fat quarter, cut:

2 strips, 2¾" × 21"; crosscut into 10 rectangles, 2¼" × 2¾" (80 total)

2 strips, 3¼" × 21"; crosscut into 8 rectangles, 2¾" × 3¼" (64 total)

2 of template A (16 total)

From *each* orange print fat eighth, cut:

1 strip, 2¾" × 21"; crosscut into 5 rectangles, 2¼" × 2¾" (20 total)

1 strip, 3¼" × 21"; crosscut into 4 rectangles, 2¾" × 3¼" (16 total)

1 of template A (4 total)

From the orange print for binding, cut:

4 strips, 2½" × 42"

PIECING THE FOUNDATION UNITS

Press all seam allowances toward each newly added piece as you go.

1 Using the patterns on page 39, make 20 copies each of units C and D, making sure to copy the patterns at 100%. Roughly cut out each pattern, leaving ¼" of paper all around the dashed outer lines. Reduce the stitch length on your sewing machine to 1.5 mm, or about 17 to 18 stitches per inch.

2 Place a white 3¼" × 3¾" rectangle on the wrong side of pattern D, covering area 1. Place an orange 2¾" × 3¼" rectangle on top of the white rectangle, right sides together. Make sure the fabrics extend at least ¼" beyond the stitching lines. Pin in place. Flip the unit over, paper side up, and sew on the line between areas 1 and 2.

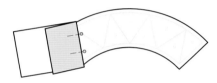

3 Open the orange rectangle and make sure it covers area 2. Press. Fold only the paper on the line between areas 2 and 3; trim the excess fabric so that it extends ¼" beyond the fold. Unfold the paper and make sure both fabrics are right side up.

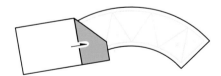

4 Pin a white 3¼" × 3¾" rectangle on top of the orange piece, right sides together. Flip the unit over, paper side up, and sew on the line between areas 2 and 3. Open the white rectangle and make sure it covers area 3. Press. Fold only the paper on the line between areas 3 and 4; trim the excess fabric so that it extends ¼" beyond the fold.

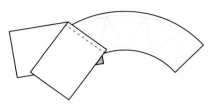

5 Continue adding white 3¼" × 3¾" rectangles and matching orange 2¾" × 3¼" rectangles in the same way until unit D is completely covered with fabric. Use a rotary cutter to trim the paper and fabrics on the dashed outer line. Carefully remove the paper. Make a total of 20 D units.

Unit D.
Make 20.

6 Repeat steps 2–5 using pattern C, orange 2¼" × 2¾" rectangles, and white 2¾" × 3¼" rectangles. Each unit begins and ends with an orange rectangle. Make a total of 20 C units.

Unit C.
Make 20.

MAKING THE BLOCKS

Press all seam allowances as indicated by the arrows.

1 Lay out one orange A piece, one white B piece, one C unit, one D unit, and one white E piece; all the orange pieces should match. Fold each piece in half and finger-press to mark the centers. Pin the B piece on top of the A piece, right sides together, matching the center and easing the fabric to fit. Sew the pieces together.

2 Repeat step 1 to sew the C unit, D unit, and E piece to complete one block. Make a total of 20 blocks measuring 7½" square, including the seam allowances.

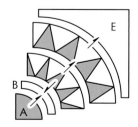

Make 20 blocks,
7½" × 7½".

ASSEMBLING THE QUILT TOP

1 Arrange the blocks in five rows of four blocks each, making sure to place blocks with matching orange fabrics next to each other as shown in the quilt assembly diagram below. Sew the blocks together in rows. Join the rows to complete the quilt top. The quilt top should measure 28½" × 35½".

2 Stitch around the perimeter of the quilt top, ⅛" from the outer edges, to lock the seams in place.

FINISHING THE QUILT

For help with the following finishing steps, go to ShopMartingale.com/HowtoQuilt for free, illustrated instructions.

1 Layer the quilt top, batting, and backing; baste the layers together. Hand or machine quilt. I free-motion quilted a variety of different motifs in each shaped piece, including swirls, spirals, and pebbles.

2 Using the orange 2½"-wide strips, bind the edges of the quilt. Add a label if desired.

Quilt assembly

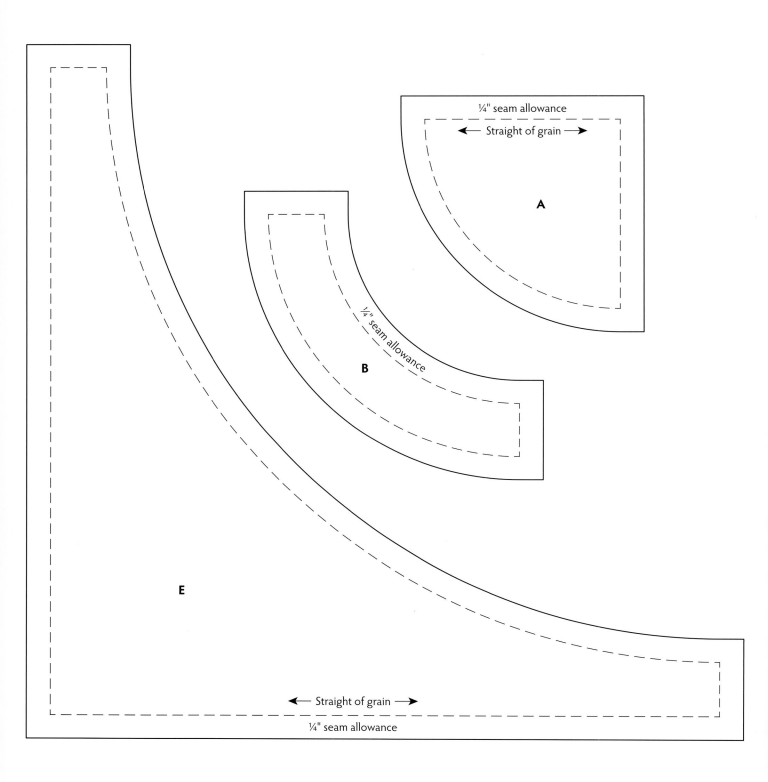

¼" seam allowance

Straight of grain

A

¼" seam allowance

B

E

Straight of grain

¼" seam allowance

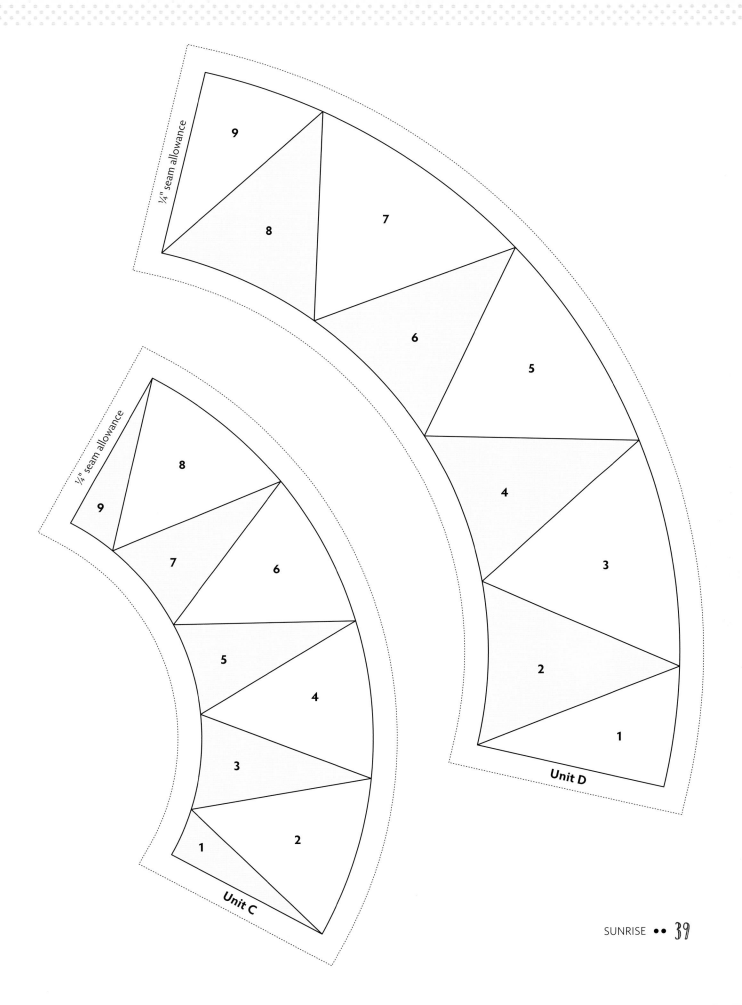

MOUNTAIN HIKING

Low-volume fabrics are perfect for backgrounds. From a distance this is a pink-and-white quilt, but come closer and it's full of color and interesting patterns.

MATERIALS

Yardage is based on 42"-wide fabric.

2¼ yards of pink print for blocks and binding

6⅔ yards *total* of assorted light prints for blocks and background

6⅞ yards of fabric for backing

81" × 89" piece of batting

Template plastic OR Triangle Squared and Perfect Rectangle rulers by Creative Grids

CUTTING

From the pink print, cut:

3 strips, 8½" × 42"

2 strips, 6½" × 42"

2 strips, 4½" × 42"

10 strips, 2½" × 42"

From the light prints, cut a *total* of:

18 rectangles, 8½" × 10"

11 rectangles, 6½" × 8"

23 rectangles, 4½" × 6"

19 rectangles, 2½" × 4"

27 squares, 8½" × 8½"

25 squares, 6½" × 6½"

49 squares, 4½" × 4½"

89 squares, 2½" × 2½"

CUTTING THE TRIANGLES

1 If you're using templates, trace patterns A–H on pages 45–47 onto template plastic and cut them out, referring to "Templates" on page 76. If you're opting for rulers, skip this step and refer to "Using Rulers Instead of Templates" on page 42.

2 Referring to "Cutting Triangles Using a Template" and using the A–D templates, cut 18 A triangles from the pink 8½"-wide strips, 11 B triangles from the pink 6½"-wide strips, 23 C triangles from the pink 4½"-wide strips, and 19 D triangles from one pink 2½"-wide strip.

3 Cut a light 8½" × 10" rectangle into two 5" × 8½" rectangles. Place the rectangles wrong sides together and align the edges. Place the E template on top of the rectangles and cut out a pair of E triangles. Notice that one triangle is a mirror image of the other. See "Cutting Triangles from Rectangles" on page 76. Repeat to cut a total of 18 pairs of E triangles.

4 Repeat step 3 using the light 6½" × 8" rectangles to cut 11 pairs of F triangles. Use the light 4½" × 6" rectangles to cut 23 pairs of G triangles. Use the light 2½" × 4" rectangles to cut 19 pairs of H triangles.

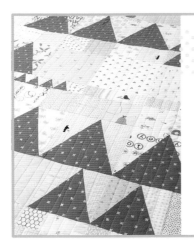

USING RULERS INSTEAD OF TEMPLATES

Making your own templates is an economical way to cut the pieces for the quilts in this project. However, special triangle rulers can make quick work of all the cutting, so if you enjoy using triangle shapes like the ones in this project, you may want to consider using a ruler instead. If you're using the Triangle Squared and Perfect Rectangle rulers, follow the instructions that come with them, and use the patterns to determine which line to use for each size of triangle.

MAKING THE BLOCKS

Press all seam allowances as indicated by the arrows.

1 Place a light E triangle on top of a pink A triangle, right sides together, aligning the raw edges and corners. Sew the triangles together. Sew a matching light E triangle to the other side of the A triangle. The second E triangle should be a mirror image of the first E triangle. Repeat to make a total of 18 A/E blocks measuring 8½" square, including the seam allowances.

Make 18 blocks,
8½" × 8½".

2 Repeat step 1 using the pink B triangles and matching pairs of light F triangles to make 11 B/F blocks measuring 6½" square. Use the pink C triangles and matching pairs of light G triangles to make 23 C/G blocks measuring 4½" square. Use the

pink D triangles and matching pairs of light H triangles to make 19 D/H blocks measuring 2½" square.

Make 11 blocks,
6½" × 6½".

Make 23 blocks,
4½" × 4½".

Make 19 blocks,
2½" × 2½".

ASSEMBLING THE QUILT TOP

1 Arrange the A/E blocks and light 8½" squares in five rows. Each row should contain a total of nine blocks and squares. Join the pieces in each row to make a row measuring 8½" × 72½", including the seam allowances. Make one of each row.

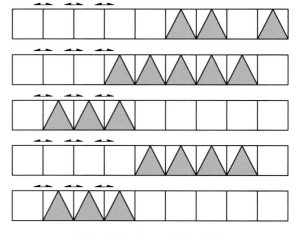

Make 1 of each row, 8½" × 72½".

2 Arrange the B/F blocks and light 6½" squares in three rows. Each row should contain a total of 12 blocks and squares. Join the pieces in each row to make a row measuring 6½" × 72½", including the seam allowances. Make one of each row.

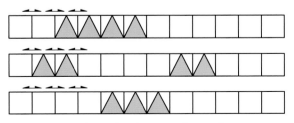

Make 1 of each row, 6½" × 72½".

3 Arrange the C/G blocks and light 4½" squares in four rows. Each row should contain a total of 18 blocks and squares. Join the pieces in each row to make a row measuring 4½" × 72½", including the seam allowances. Make one of each row.

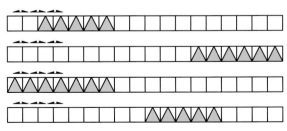

Make 1 of each row, 4½" × 72½".

4 Arrange the D/H blocks and light 2½" squares in three rows. Each row should contain a total of 36 blocks and squares. Join the pieces in each row to make a row measuring 2½" × 72½", including the seam allowances. Make one of each row.

Make 1 of each row, 2½" × 72½".

5 Lay out the rows from steps 1–4 as shown in the quilt assembly diagram below. Sew the rows together to complete the quilt top. The quilt top should measure 72½" × 80½".

6 Stitch around the perimeter of the quilt top, ⅛" from the outer edges, to lock the seams in place.

FINISHING THE QUILT

For help with the following finishing steps, go to ShopMartingale.com/HowtoQuilt for free, illustrated instructions.

1 Layer the quilt top, batting, and backing; baste the layers together. Hand or machine quilt. I used a walking foot to quilt parallel straight vertical lines across the quilt.

2 Using the remaining pink 2½"-wide strips, bind the edges of the quilt. Add a label if desired.

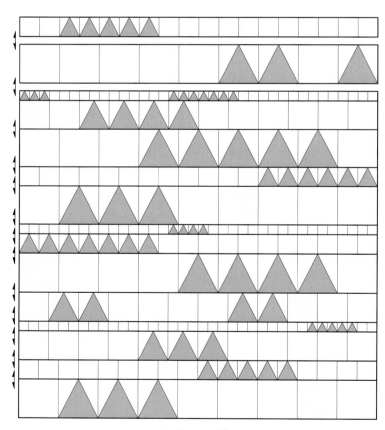

Quilt assembly

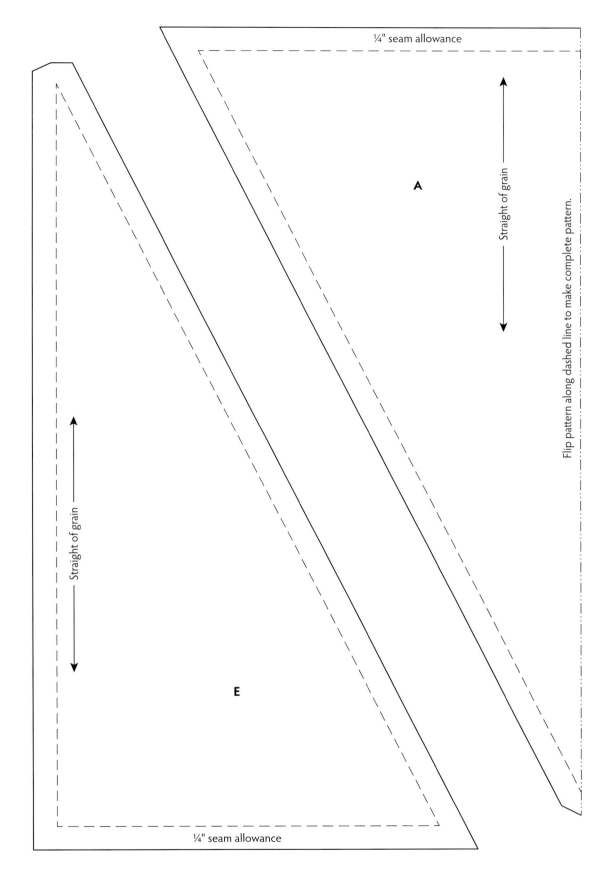

¼" seam allowance

A

Straight of grain

Flip pattern along dashed line to make complete pattern.

Straight of grain

E

¼" seam allowance

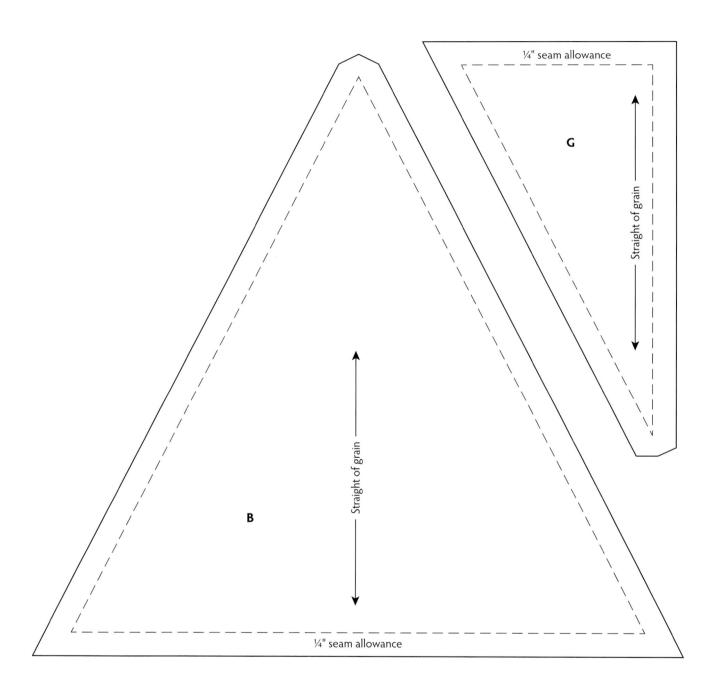

¼" seam allowance

Straight of grain

G

B

Straight of grain

¼" seam allowance

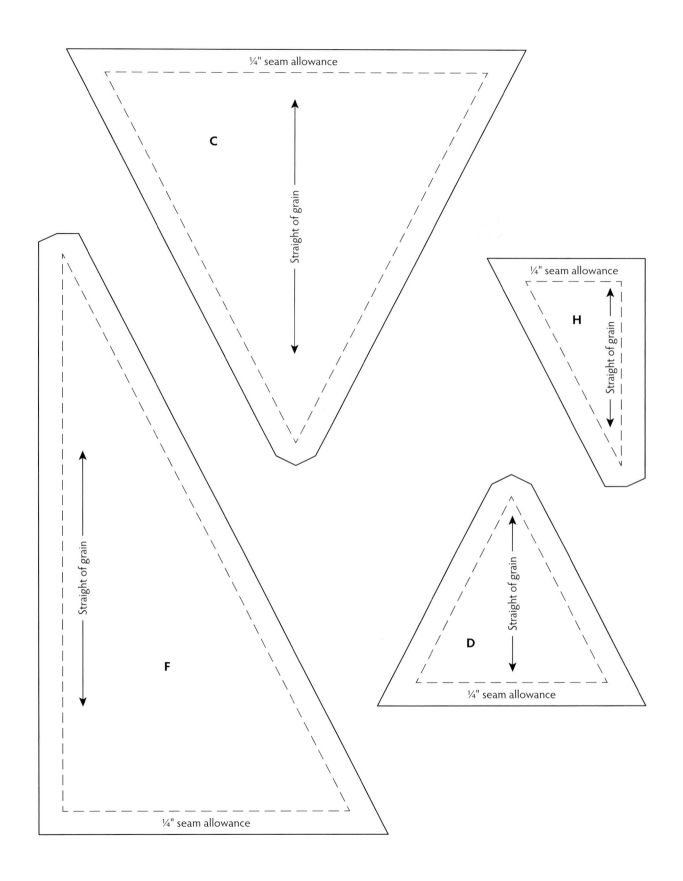

¼" seam allowance

C

Straight of grain

¼" seam allowance

H

Straight of grain

Straight of grain

F

¼" seam allowance

Straight of grain

D

¼" seam allowance

SHIMMER

Half-square triangles might be the simplest of blocks, but this design has maximum impact. I made the center block a bright contrasting color.

MATERIALS

Yardage is based on 42"-wide fabric.

2 yards of white solid for blocks and border
64 squares, 5" × 5", of assorted gray prints for blocks
8 squares, 5" × 5", of assorted yellow prints for blocks
½ yard of gray print for binding
1 strip, 2½" × 21", of yellow print for binding
3½ yards of fabric for backing
59" × 59" square of batting

CUTTING

From the white solid, cut:
10 strips, 5" × 42"; crosscut into 72 squares, 5" × 5"
6 strips, 2½" × 42"

From the gray print for binding, cut:
6 strips, 2½" × 42"

FABRIC VARIETY

I cut gray and yellow squares from fabrics in my stash and scrap basket, but if your stash doesn't yield the variety you want, try 5" squares from charm packs instead.

MAKING THE BLOCKS

Press all seam allowances as indicated by the arrows.

1. Referring to "Half-Square-Triangle Units" on page 78, pair a white square with a gray square to make two half-square triangles. Trim to 4½" square. Make 128 gray units. Use the yellow and remaining white squares to make 16 yellow units.

Make 128 units.   Make 16 units.

2. Arrange 16 gray units in four rows of four units each, orienting the units in adjoining rows in opposite directions as shown. Sew the units in each row together. Join the rows to complete one gray block. Make a total of eight blocks measuring 16½" square, including the seam allowances.

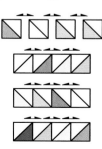

Make 8 blocks, 16½" × 16½".

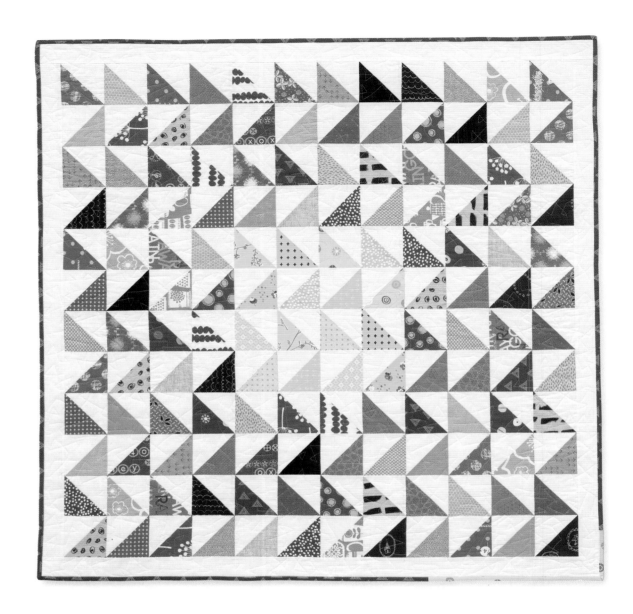

3 Repeat step 2 using the yellow units to make one block measuring 16½" square, including the seam allowances.

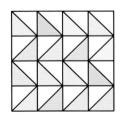

Make 1 block,
16½" × 16½".

ASSEMBLING THE QUILT TOP

1 Arrange the blocks in three rows of three blocks each, placing the yellow block in the center as shown in the quilt assembly diagram on page 51. Sew the blocks together into rows. Join the rows to complete the quilt-top center. The quilt top should measure 48½" square, including the seam allowances.

2 Sew the white 2½"-wide strips together end to end. From the pieced strip, cut two 48½"-long strips and two 52½"-long strips. Sew the 48½"-long strips to opposite sides of the quilt top. Sew the 52½"-long strips to the top and bottom of the quilt top. The quilt should measure 52½" square.

FINISHING THE QUILT

Go to ShopMartingale.com/HowtoQuilt for free, illustrated instructions of these finishing techniques.

1 Layer the quilt top, batting, and backing; baste the layers together. Hand or machine quilt. I free-motion quilted a pattern of overlapping triangles across the quilt.

2 Referring to "Binding with a Contrast Strip" on page 62, use the gray 2½"-wide strips and the yellow 2½" × 21" strip to bind the edges of the quilt. Add a label if desired.

PERFECT POINTS

To get perfect triangle points when joining rows, start by matching all the seam intersections. Using thin pins, place a pin on either side of the seam. Then use a scant ¼" seam allowance to sew a few basting stitches, checking to make sure that the seams match perfectly. If they don't, remove the basting stitches, reposition the seams, and try again. When all the points match, sew the entire row together using a regular stitch length.

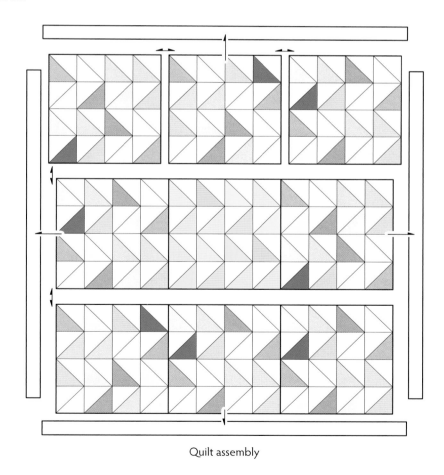

Quilt assembly

MELLOW

Fabrics from opposite sides of the color wheel can be quite loud and overpowering. Tone them down by using pastel shades, and you'll have a calming quilt to wrap yourself in.

MATERIALS

Yardage is based on 42"-wide fabric.

⅝ yard *each* of 4 assorted orange prints for blocks
⅝ yard *each* of 4 assorted aqua prints for blocks
⅝ yard *each* of 4 assorted pink prints for blocks
⅝ yard of blue print for binding
3¾ yards of fabric for backing
65" × 79" piece of batting

CUTTING

From *each* of 2 orange prints, 1 aqua print, and
1 pink print, cut:
3 strips, 2½" × 42"; crosscut into 6 strips,
    2½" × 14½" (24 total)
4 strips, 2" × 42"; crosscut into 8 strips, 2" × 14½"
    (32 total)
1 strip, 1½" × 42"; crosscut into 2 strips, 1½" × 14½"
    (8 total)

From *each* of 1 orange print, 1 aqua print, and 2 pink
prints, cut:
2 strips, 2½" × 42"; crosscut into 3 strips,
    2½" × 14½" (12 total)
4 strips, 2" × 42"; crosscut into 8 strips, 2" × 14½"
    (32 total)
2 strips, 1½" × 42"; crosscut into 4 strips,
    1½" × 14½" (16 total)

From *each* of 1 orange print, 2 aqua prints, and
1 pink print, cut:
3 strips, 2½" × 42"; crosscut into 6 strips,
    2½" × 14½" (24 total)
2 strips, 2" × 42"; crosscut into 4 strips, 2" × 14½"
    (16 total)
2 strips, 1½" × 42"; crosscut into 4 strips,
    1½" × 14½" (16 total)

From the blue print for binding, cut:
7 strips, 2½" × 42"

MAKING THE BLOCKS

Press all seam allowances as indicated by the arrows.

1 Sort the strips into 20 sets, each containing
   three matching 2½" × 14½" strips, four
matching 2" × 14½" strips, and two matching
1½" × 14½" strips. Make sure each set has one
group of strips in each of the three colors: pink,
orange, and aqua.

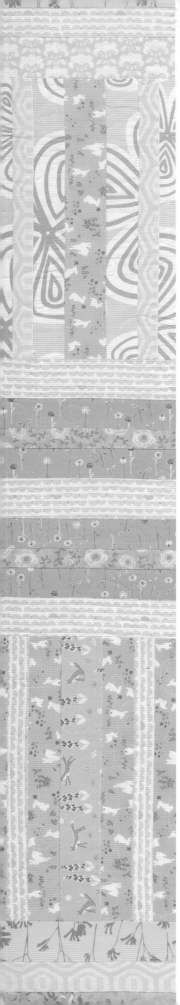

MIXING PRINT STYLES

To give a quilt made only of long strips some excitement and movement, consider including a variety of print styles. Here I used stripes, geometrics, and large-scale organic prints to really pack a punch.

2 Arrange the strips from one set as shown. Sew the strips together along their long edges to complete one block. Make 20 blocks measuring 14½" square, including the seam allowances.

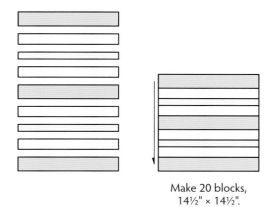

Make 20 blocks, 14½" × 14½".

ASSEMBLING THE QUILT TOP

1 Arrange the blocks in five rows of four blocks each, rotating every other block as shown in the quilt assembly diagram below. Sew the blocks together into rows. Join the rows to complete the quilt top. The quilt top should measure 56½" × 70½".

2 Stitch around the perimeter of the quilt top, ⅛" from the outer edges, to lock the seams in place.

FINISHING THE QUILT

For help with the following finishing steps, go to ShopMartingale.com/HowtoQuilt for free, illustrated instructions.

1 Layer the quilt top, batting, and backing; baste the layers together. Hand or machine quilt. I free-motion quilted wavy vertical lines mixed with circles across the quilt top.

2 Using the blue 2½"-wide strips, bind the edges of the quilt. Add a label if desired.

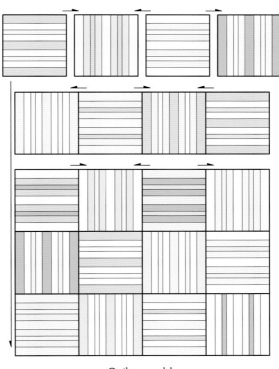

Quilt assembly

PETUNIA PATCH

Gardens are the best place to find interesting color combinations, and each season will give you new inspiration. Pink and green will always be one of my favorite combinations.

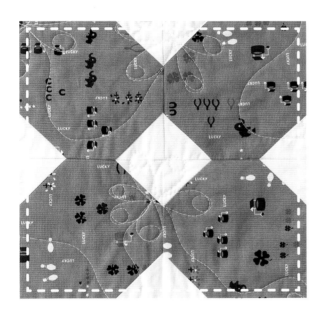

MATERIALS

Yardage is based on 42"-wide fabric.

3⅛ yards of white solid for background

24 rectangles, 2" × 9½", of assorted green prints for Stem blocks

25 squares, 10" × 10", of assorted pink prints for Flower blocks

⅝ yard of pink print for binding

1 strip, 2½" × 20", of green print for binding

4½ yards of fabric for backing

76" × 76" square of batting

CUTTING

From the white solid, cut:
16 strips, 2" × 42"; crosscut into 300 squares, 2" × 2"
12 strips, 4¼" × 42"; crosscut into 48 rectangles,
   4¼" × 9½"
7 strips, 2¾" × 42"

From *each* of the pink squares, cut:
4 squares, 5" × 5" (100 total)

From the pink print for binding, cut:
7 strips, 2½" × 42"

MAKING THE STEM BLOCKS

Sew white 4¼" × 9½" rectangles to opposite sides of a green 2" × 9½" rectangle to complete a Stem block. Make 24 blocks measuring 9½" square, including the seam allowances. Press all seam allowances as indicated by the arrows.

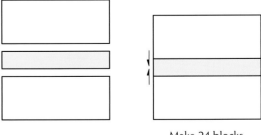

Make 24 blocks,
9½" × 9½".

MAKING THE FLOWER BLOCKS

1 Refer to "Triangle Corners" on page 77. Sew white 2" squares on three corners of a pink 5" square as shown to make a unit. Repeat to make four identical units measuring 5" square. Press the seam allowances on two of the units toward the white triangles. Press the seam allowances on the other two units toward the pink square. Make a total of 25 sets of four identical units.

2 Arrange four identical units from step 1 in two rows, placing units with opposite pressed seam allowances adjacent to each other. Sew the units together into rows. Join the rows to complete a Flower block. Make 25 blocks measuring 9½" square, including the seam allowances.

Make 2 of each unit,
5" × 5".

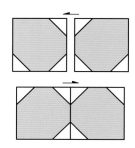
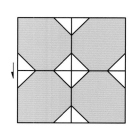

Make 25 blocks,
9½" × 9½".

ASSEMBLING THE QUILT TOP

1 Arrange the blocks in seven rows of seven blocks each, alternating the Stem and Flower blocks as shown in the quilt assembly diagram below. Sew the blocks together into rows. Join the rows to complete the quilt-top center, which should measure 63½" square, including the seam allowances.

2 Sew the white 2¾"-wide strips together end to end. From the pieced strip, cut two 63½"-long and two 68"-long strips. Sew the 63½"-long strips to opposite sides of the quilt top. Sew the 68"-long strips to the top and bottom of the quilt top. The quilt top should measure 68" square.

FINISHING THE QUILT

For help with the following finishing steps, go to ShopMartingale.com/HowtoQuilt for free, illustrated instructions.

1 Layer the quilt top, batting, and backing; baste the layers together. Hand or machine quilt. I free-motion quilted an allover whirligig flower pattern across the quilt.

2 Referring to "Binding with a Contrast Strip" on page 62, use the pink 2½"-wide strips and the green 2½" × 20" strip to bind the edges of the quilt. Add a label if desired.

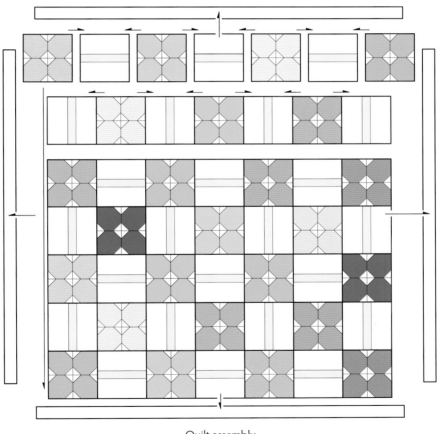

Quilt assembly

BETWEEN THE LINES

This pattern makes the ideal baby quilt. It looks great in any complementary color combination, not just the blue and orange shown here.

MATERIALS

Yardage is based on 42"-wide fabric.

1⅛ yards of white solid for background
⅓ yard of blue print for strips and binding
1 yard of orange print for strips and binding
2¾ yards of fabric for backing
45" × 51" piece of batting

CUTTING

From the white solid, cut:
13 strips, 2½" × 42"; crosscut into:
    10 strips, 2½" × 38½"
    10 rectangles, 2½" × 8½"

From the blue print, cut:
3 strips, 2½" × 42"; crosscut into 9 rectangles,
    2½" × 8½"
1 strip, 2½" × 25"

From the orange print, cut:
4 strips, 2½" × 42"
8 strips, 2½" × 38½"

ASSEMBLING THE QUILT TOP

Press all seam allowances as indicated by the arrows.

1 Starting and ending with a white rectangle, join the white and blue 2½" × 8½" rectangles along their long edges, alternating them as shown to make the middle section. The section should measure 8½" × 38½", including the seam allowances.

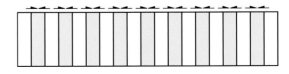

Make 1 section,
8½" × 38½".

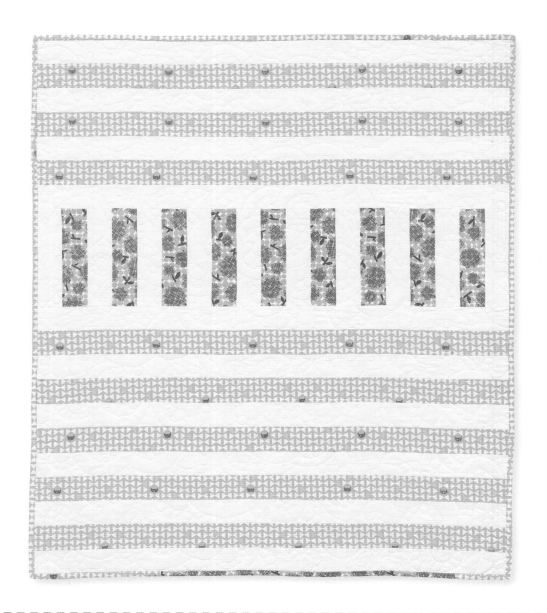

BINDING WITH A CONTRAST STRIP

An alternative to making a completely scrappy binding is to add a contrast strip to a single-fabric binding, as shown above. The length of the contrast strip is entirely up to you. I use a length of anywhere between 10" and 40", depending on the size of the quilt and where I want the contrast strip to be. I make the binding by joining all the matching binding strips and then sewing the contrast strip to one end.

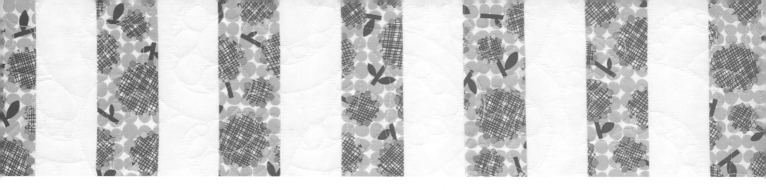

2 Starting and ending with a white strip, join four white strips and three orange 2½" × 38½" strips, alternating them as shown to make the top section. The section should measure 14½" × 38½", including the seam allowances.

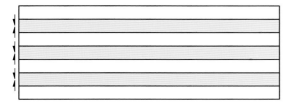

Make 1 section,
14½" × 38½".

3 Starting and ending with a white strip, join six white strips and five orange 2½" × 38½" strips, alternating them as shown to make the bottom section. The section should measure 22½" × 38½", including the seam allowances.

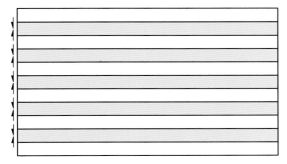

Make 1 section,
22½" × 38½".

4 Sew the top and bottom sections to opposite sides of the middle section to complete the quilt top. The quilt top should measure 38½" × 44½".

5 Stitch around the perimeter of the quilt top, ⅛" from the outer edges, to lock the seams in place.

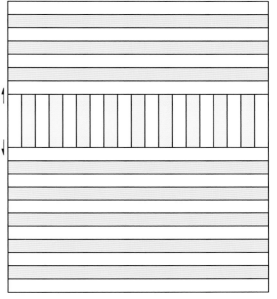

Quilt assembly

FINISHING THE QUILT

Go to ShopMartingale.com/HowtoQuilt for free, illustrated instructions of these finishing techniques.

1 Layer the quilt top, batting, and backing; baste the layers together. Hand or machine quilt. I free-motion quilted an allover circular pattern across the quilt.

2 Referring to "Binding with a Contrast Strip" on page 62, use the orange 2½"-wide strips and the blue 2½" × 25" strip to bind the edges of the quilt. Add a label if desired.

TRIANGLE TREES

FINISHED QUILT: 66" × 74½" | FINISHED BLOCK: 13⅞" × 16"

The pine trees in the plantations surrounding our little town were the inspiration for this quilt. I echoed the triangular shape of the pine trees by making each one from multiple triangles.

MATERIALS

Yardage is based on 42"-wide fabric.

4⅜ yards of white solid for background

1 rectangle, 10" × 13", of brown print for blocks

15 rectangles, 10" × 13", of assorted green prints for blocks

⅓ yard *total* of assorted brown prints for blocks

1 rectangle, 2⅞" × 4½", of green print for blocks

⅝ yard of brown print for binding

1 strip, 2½" × 42", of green print for binding

4¾ yards of fabric for backing

74" × 83" piece of batting

Template plastic *OR* 60° triangle ruler

CUTTING

From the white solid, cut:

10 strips, 4½" × 42"; crosscut 6 *of the strips* into 32 rectangles, 4½" × 6¼"

4 strips, 12½" × 42"; crosscut into 16 rectangles, 10" × 12½"

19 strips, 2½" × 42"; crosscut 12 *of the strips* into:
12 rectangles, 2½" × 16½"
12 rectangles, 2½" × 14⅜"

From the brown rectangle, cut:

2 rectangles, 4½" × 13"

From *each* of the 15 assorted green rectangles, cut:
2 rectangles, 4½" × 13" (30 total)

From the assorted brown prints, cut a *total* of:
15 rectangles, 2⅞" × 4½"
9 squares, 2½" × 2½"

From the brown print for binding, cut:
7 strips, 2½" × 42"

CUTTING THE TRIANGLES

1 Referring to "Templates" on page 76, trace patterns A and B on pages 69 and 70 onto template plastic and cut them out. You can skip this step if you're using a ruler.

2 Refer to "Cutting Triangles Using a Template" on page 76. Use the white 4½" × 42" strips and template A to cut a total of 48 A triangles. From *each* of the brown and green 4½" × 13" rectangles, cut three A triangles. You'll have six A triangles from each of these brown and green fabrics.

3 Place two white 10" × 12½" rectangles wrong sides together and align the edges. Place the B template on top of the rectangles and cut a pair of B triangles. Notice that one triangle is a mirror image of the other. Rotate the B template and cut out a second pair of B triangles. See "Cutting Triangles from Rectangles" on page 76. Repeat to cut a total of 16 pairs of B triangles.

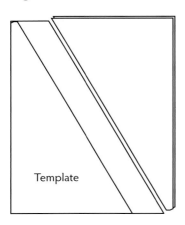

Template

USING A RULER

Making your own templates is an economical way to cut the pieces for this project. However, using a special triangle ruler can make quick work of the cutting, so if you like using 60° triangle shapes, you may want to consider using a ruler instead. If you're using a ruler, follow the instructions that come with it and measure to the 4½" line.

MAKING THE BLOCKS

Press all seam allowances as indicated by the arrows.

1 Arrange six matching green A triangles and three white A triangles in three rows. Sew the triangles together into rows. Join the rows to make a triangular unit. Make 15 units.

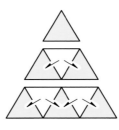
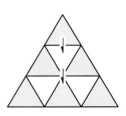

Make 15.

2 Place a white B triangle on top of a unit from step 1, right sides together, aligning the raw edges and corners. Sew the triangle and unit together. Sew a white B triangle to the other side of the unit. The second B triangle should be a mirror image of the first. Repeat to make a total of 15 green units measuring 12½" × 14⅜", including the seam allowances.

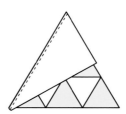
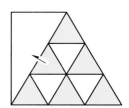
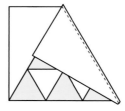
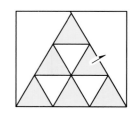

Make 15 units, 12½" × 14⅜".

- -

3 Repeat steps 1 and 2 using the brown A triangles instead of the green A triangles to make one brown unit.

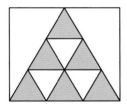

Make 1 unit,
12½" × 14⅜".

4 Sew white 4½" × 6¼" rectangles to opposite sides of a brown 2⅞" × 4½" rectangle to make a trunk unit. Make 15 units measuring 4½" × 14⅜", including the seam allowances.

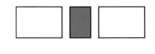 

Make 15 units,
4½" × 14⅜".

5 Sew white 4½" × 6¼" rectangles to opposite sides of the green 2⅞" × 4½" rectangle to make one trunk unit measuring 4½" × 14⅜", including the seam allowances.

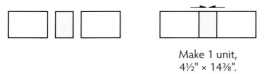

Make 1 unit,
4½" × 14⅜".

6 Join a green triangle unit from step 2 and a unit from step 4 to complete one block. Make 15 green blocks measuring 14⅜" × 16½", including the seam allowances.

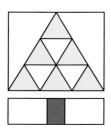
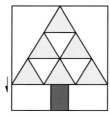

Make 15 blocks,
14⅜" × 16½".

7 Sew the brown triangle unit from step 3 to the unit from step 5 to complete one brown block measuring 14⅜" × 16½", including the seam allowances.

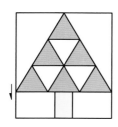

Make 1 block,
14⅜" × 16½".

ASSEMBLING THE QUILT TOP

1 Sew three brown 2½" squares and four white 2½" × 14⅜" rectangles together to make a sashing strip. Make three sashing strips measuring 2½" × 62", including the seam allowances.

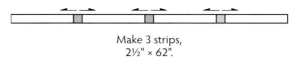

Make 3 strips,
2½" × 62".

2 Sew four tree blocks and three white 2½" × 16½" rectangles together, alternating them as shown. Make four rows measuring 16½" × 62", including the seam allowances. Refer to the photo on page 67 for placement of the brown tree block.

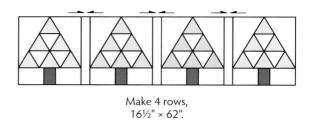

Make 4 rows,
16½" × 62".

3 Join the block rows and sashing strips as shown in the quilt assembly diagram on page 69 to complete the quilt-top center. The quilt top should measure 62" × 70½", including the seam allowances.

4 Sew the remaining white 2½"-wide strips together end to end. From the pieced strip, cut two 70½"-long and two 66"-long strips. Sew the 70½"-long strips to opposite sides of the quilt top. Sew the 66"-long strips to the top and bottom of the quilt top to complete the border. The quilt top should measure 66" × 74½".

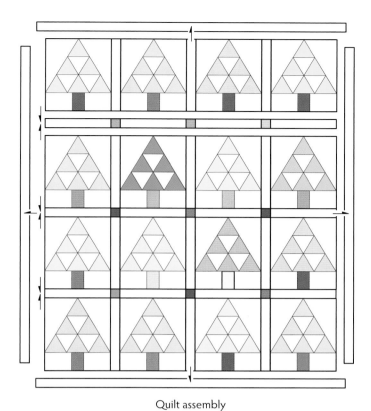

Quilt assembly

FINISHING THE QUILT

Go to ShopMartingale.com/HowtoQuilt for free, illustrated instructions of these finishing techniques.

1 Layer the quilt top, batting, and backing; baste the layers together. Hand or machine quilt. I free-motion quilted an allover leaf pattern across the quilt.

2 Referring to "Binding with a Contrast Strip" on page 62, use the brown 2½"-wide strips and the green 2½"-wide strip to bind the edges of the quilt. Add a label if desired.

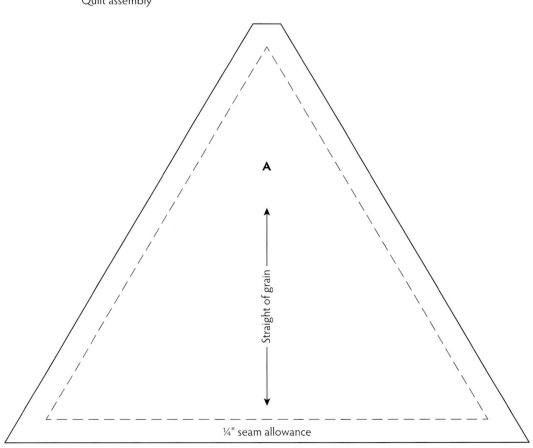

A

Straight of grain

¼" seam allowance

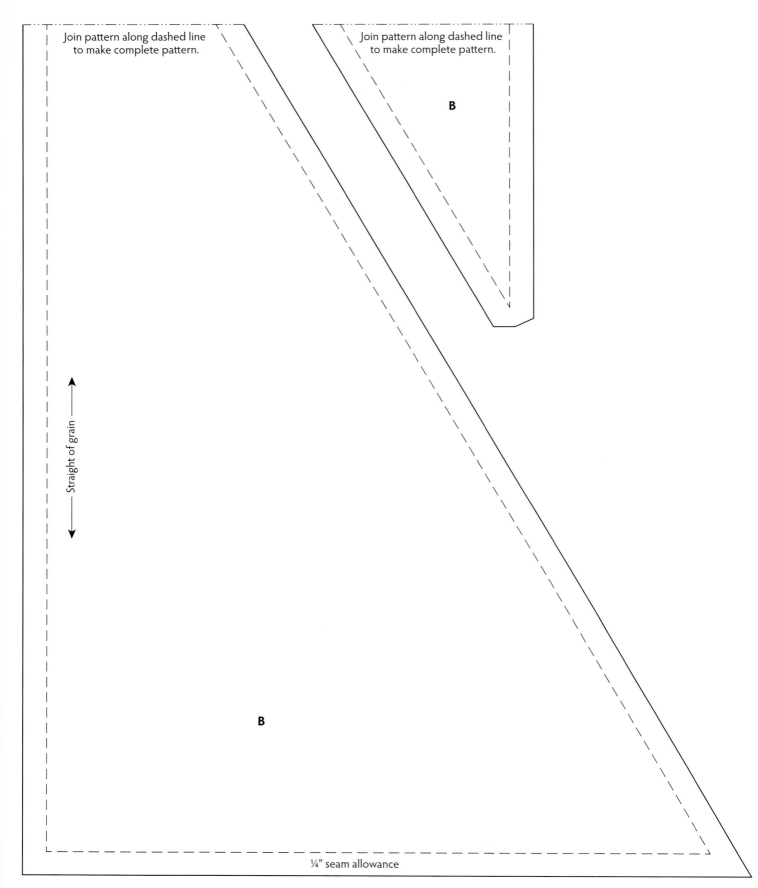

Join pattern along dashed line to make complete pattern.

Join pattern along dashed line to make complete pattern.

B

Straight of grain

B

¼" seam allowance

ADD IT UP

FINISHED QUILT: 68½" × 68½" | FINISHED BLOCK: 12" × 12"

Three simple blocks make up this fun design that features a classic red, white, and blue color scheme.

CUTTING

From the white print, cut:
8 strips, 5" × 42"; crosscut into 52 squares, 5" × 5"
12 strips, 4½" × 42"; crosscut into 96 squares,
    4½" × 4½"

From the red print, cut:
6 strips, 4½" × 42"; crosscut into:
    9 rectangles, 4½" × 12½"
    22 squares, 4½" × 4½"

From the blue print, cut:
8 strips, 5" × 42"; crosscut into 52 squares, 5" × 5"
5 strips, 4½" × 42"; crosscut into:
    12 rectangles, 4½" × 12½"
    4 squares, 4½" × 4½"
8 strips, 2½" × 42"

MATERIALS

Yardage is based on 42"-wide fabric.

2⅞ yards of white print for blocks and pieced border
⅞ yard of red print for blocks
2⅝ yards of blue print for blocks, pieced border, and
    binding
4⅜ yards of fabric for backing
77" × 77" square of batting

CHANGE THE SIZE

Many quilts in this book can be made bigger or smaller simply by adding or taking away blocks or rows. I like to make extra blocks so that I can play around with the layout. Then I use the extra blocks to make cushions or mini-quilts.

MAKING BLOCK A

Press all seam allowances as indicated by the arrows.

1 Sew white 4½" squares to opposite sides of a red 4½" square to make a unit. Make 22 units measuring 4½" × 12½", including the seam allowances.

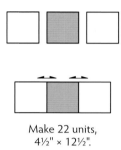

Make 22 units,
4½" × 12½".

2 Sew units from step 1 to the top and bottom of a red 4½" × 12½" rectangle to complete one A block. Make nine blocks measuring 12½" square, including the seam allowances. Set aside the remaining units from step 1 for the B blocks.

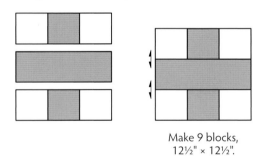

Make 9 blocks,
12½" × 12½".

MAKING BLOCK B

1 Referring to "Half-Square-Triangle Units" on page 78, pair a white 5" square with a blue 5" square to make two half-square-triangle units. Trim the units to measure 4½" square. Make 104 units.

Make 104 units.

2 Sew half-square-triangle units to opposite sides of a white 4½" square to make a unit. Make 52 units measuring 4½" × 12½", including the seam allowances.

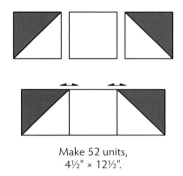

Make 52 units,
4½" × 12½".

3 Lay out two units from step 2 (above) and one unit from step 1 of "Making Block A" (at left) as shown. Join the units to make one B block. Make four blocks measuring 12½" square, including the seam allowances. Set aside the remaining units from step 2 of "Making Block B" for making the C blocks and pieced border.

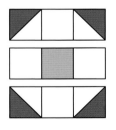 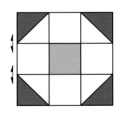

Make 4 blocks,
12½" × 12½".

MAKING BLOCK C

Sew two units from step 2 of "Making Block B" to the top and bottom of a blue 4½" × 12½" rectangle to complete one C block. Make 12 blocks measuring 12½" square, including the seam allowances.

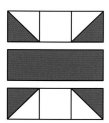 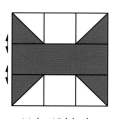

Make 12 blocks,
12½" × 12½".

QUILTING

I machine quilt my quilts on a domestic sewing machine. There's something magical about seeing a quilt top transform into a quilt. With just your home sewing machine, you can quilt straight lines using a walking foot, employ free-motion techniques, or use a combination of both.

ASSEMBLING THE QUILT TOP

1 Arrange the A, B, and C blocks in five rows of five blocks each as shown in the quilt assembly diagram. Sew the blocks together into rows. Join the rows to complete the quilt-top center. The quilt top should measure 60½" square, including the seam allowances.

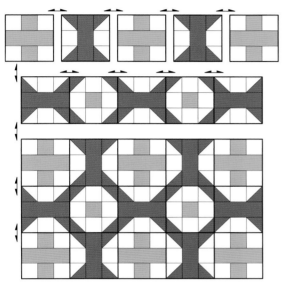

Quilt assembly

2 Join five of the remaining units from step 2 of "Making Block B," rotating every other unit as shown to make one border strip. Make four strips measuring 4½" × 60½", including the seam allowances.

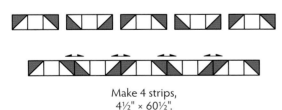

Make 4 strips,
4½" × 60½".

3 Sew border strips from step 2 to the top and bottom of the quilt top. Sew blue 4½" squares to both ends of the two remaining border strips. Sew these borders to opposite sides of the quilt top. The quilt top should measure 68½" square.

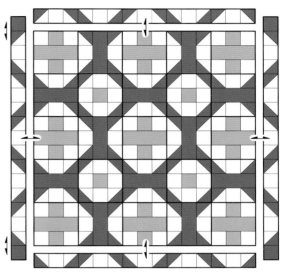

Add borders

FINISHING THE QUILT

For help with the following finishing steps, go to ShopMartingale.com/HowtoQuilt for free, illustrated instructions.

1 Layer the quilt top, batting, and backing; baste the layers together. Hand or machine quilt. I free-motion quilted an allover wave pattern across the quilt.

2 Using the blue 2½"-wide strips, bind the edges of the quilt. Add a label if desired.

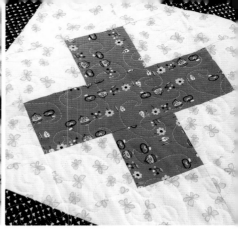

GENERAL INSTRUCTIONS

As you create your quilts, there are some basic bits of information to keep in mind. I've included my best hints and tips here. You can also visit ShopMartingale.com/HowtoQuilt for free, downloadable information.

FABRIC AND THREAD

All the projects in this book are based on fabric with 42" of usable width. I used 100% cotton fabrics for all the projects, and 100% cotton thread for all my piecing and quilting. I love Aurifil 50-weight thread and find it's perfect for all aspects of quilting.

TEMPLATES

Several of these projects use templates. The pattern for each template can be found after the project instructions. To make a template, place template plastic over each pattern piece and trace with a fine-line marker, making sure to trace the lines exactly. Use utility scissors to cut out the templates, cutting exactly on the drawn line. Use the following instructions to cut triangles with a template or starting with a rectangle.

Cutting Triangles Using a Template

Align the blunt point on the template with one long raw edge of the fabric strip. Align the base of the triangle with the opposite raw edge. Trace along the template's angled edges and cut along the lines. You can use scissors or lay a rotary-cutting ruler along the line and cut with a rotary cutter.

Rotate the template 180° and position it next to the angled cut edge, making sure the top and bottom of the triangle align with the fabric edges. Cut a second triangle. Repeat for the required number of triangles.

Cutting Triangles from Rectangles

Place two rectangles of fabric wrong sides together, aligning the top, bottom, and side edges. Place the template on top of the rectangles, aligning the bottom and side edges with the edges of the rectangles. Trace along the angled edge of the template. To cut out a pair of triangles, use scissors or lay a rotary-cutting ruler along the line and cut with a rotary cutter. Notice that one triangle is a mirror image of the other.

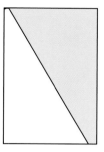

SEAM ALLOWANCES

A ¼" seam allowance is used throughout this book. Even if you use a ¼" presser foot on your machine, it's worth checking to make sure you're sewing an accurate ¼" seam allowance.

To check your seam allowance, sew three 2½"-wide strips together and press. The finished unit should measure 6½" wide. If it measures more than 6½", increase the seam allowances by a thread's width (0.5 mm) or two. If it measures less than 6½", make the seam allowances correspondingly narrower. Keep testing until you achieve a seam allowance that is exactly ¼" wide.

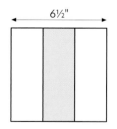

PRESSING

My only rule for pressing seam allowances is to do what you prefer. Seam allowances can be pressed to one side or open. I tend to do a bit of both, and throughout this book I indicate the pressing direction I recommend for each seam allowance.

I think pressing the seam allowances open makes a flatter quilt top, especially when sewing half-square triangles and triangle corners (sometimes called half-square corners). But pressing to one side is quicker and can make the seams match more precisely. If there's sashing in the quilt, I press the seam allowances to one side, usually toward the sashing. In quilts with mainly straight lines or in simple quilts I want to make quickly, I press the seam allowances to one side.

QUICK PIECING TECHNIQUES

After you've cut the pieces, it's time to sew them together. Here are several techniques to make your piecing faster and more accurate.

Chain Piecing

Chain piecing saves time and thread. Instead of sewing together just two pieces of fabric at a time, get a whole pile ready to sew. After you have sewn the first pair, leave the presser foot down, feed the next pair under the foot, and keep sewing. When all the pieces in the pile are sewn, lift the presser foot, cut the thread, and then cut the chains of thread between the pairs.

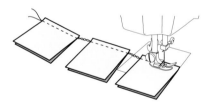

Triangle Corners

1 Use a sharp pencil to draw a diagonal line from corner to corner across the wrong side of a corner square. Place the marked square on the corner of a larger square (or rectangle), right sides together, and sew one thread width away from the drawn line on the seam-allowance side.

2 Fold the resulting triangle over the seamline to check that it matches the edges of the larger square (or rectangle), and adjust the stitching line if necessary. Return the corner square to the sewing position and trim the corner, leaving a ¼"-wide seam allowance. Fold the resulting triangle outward and press the seam allowances in the direction indicated in the project instructions.

To save time drawing lines on the squares, place a strip of painter's or masking tape on the sewing-machine bed as a guide for positioning the squares. Start sewing at the outer corner and align the square's opposite corner with the edge of the masking tape.

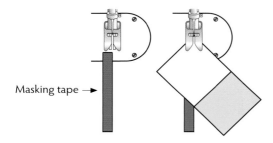

Masking tape →

ROTARY CUTTING

Rotary cutting is the most accurate way to cut fabric. Having rulers of various sizes at hand will simplify the cutting process, but you can manage with just a couple of different lengths. It's worth investing in both a ruler and mat that are at least 24" long to make cutting strips from the width of the fabric easy. To minimize fabric waste, cut the longest pieces from your strips first and the shortest pieces last.

Half-Square-Triangle Units

A number of the projects use half-square-triangle units. To make half-square-triangle units, start with squares ⅞" larger than the finished size of the half-square triangle. I prefer to trim my half-square-triangle units to make sure they're the correct size, so I cut my squares 1" larger than the required finished size. All the quilts in this book have you do the same and then trim the units to the required size. I like to use a Bloc Loc ruler to trim the half-square-triangle units, but of course you can trim them using any square ruler. I've been known to trim the units to the wrong size on more than one occasion, so now I use painter's tape or washi crafting tape to mark the size of the unit on my ruler.

1 To make a half-square-triangle unit, you'll need two same-sized squares of contrasting colors. With a sharp pencil, draw a line from corner to corner across the wrong side of the lighter fabric square.

2 Place the squares right sides together and sew ¼" from each side of the drawn line. Cut the units apart along the drawn diagonal line.

3 Press the seam allowances in the direction indicated in the project instructions. Trim the units to the required size.

SASHING AND BORDERS

In this book, the exact measurements for sashing and borders are given in each of the project instructions, but it's a good idea to measure the quilt before attaching the borders to ensure that the quilt lies flat and straight. Measure the length of the pieced quilt top from raw edge to raw edge in two different places and average the measurements. Cut the side borders this length, which includes a ½" seam allowance. Mark the centers of the quilt top and borders. Sew the borders in place, matching the center point and both ends. Press the seam allowances as directed.

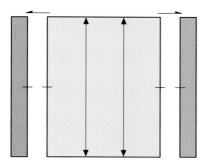

Measure the length in two places; match the centers.

Measure the width of the quilt top, including the side borders, in the same way. Cut and attach the borders as before. Press the seam allowances as directed.

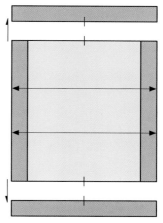

Include the borders in the width measurement.

ACKNOWLEDGMENTS

Thanks to my husband, Chris, and my girls, Grace, Amelia, Eva, and Olive, for believing in me and supporting me, for all your help with choosing fabrics, and for loving the quilts I make for you.

Thank you to the following fabric manufacturers for providing me with beautiful fabric: Moda, Riley Blake Designs, and Ella Blue. Thank you to Aurifil for the wonderful thread.

Thank you to everyone at Martingale for your encouragement, support, and professionalism.

ABOUT THE AUTHOR

Kate learned to sew clothes at the age of 12 and has been sewing ever since. She is the author of Striking Strip Quilts and Strip Savvy (Martingale, 2016 and 2014, respectively), and she has also contributed to several collaborative Martingale books. She lives in the southwest of Western Australia with her husband and four girls. You can visit her blog at KateHendersonQuilts.com and find her on Instagram at KateHendersonQuilts.